A Tangled Ball of Yarn

A Tangled Ball of Yarn

THE LIFELINE

SUSIE GLADNEY-LEE

Amy L. Deanes

Superior Publishing LLC.

CONTENTS

DEDICATION	viii
notes	1
FOREWORD	2
1　A BALL OF YARN	6
2　SACRIFICES	10
3　TEARS	13
4　FAMILY STRINGS PULL HARD	16
5　LIVING WITH TWO MEN	19
6　A VISIT FROM HELL	23
7　THE LORD IS MY SHEPHERD	27
8　TRIUMPH OVER TRAGEDY	30

CONTENTS

AFTERWORD 33

ABOUT THE AUTHOR 34

Copyright © 2024 by SUSIE GLADNEY-LEE
ISBN/SKU978-1-953056-49-8
EISBN978-1-953056-45-0

All rights reserved. No part of this book may be reproduced in any manner whatsoever without written permission except in the case of brief quotations embodied in critical articles and reviews.

Superior Publishing LLC, 2024
662-295-9893

I would like to dedicate this book to my lovely family
Especially my two beautiful daughters

Foreword
Reverend Orlando R. Richmond, Sr.

Afterword
Christon Robinson

FOREWORD

Sometimes speaking the truth hurts. Sometimes speaking the truth helps the healing process. And then there are times when speaking the truth does both.

There are very few literary works which have ever been written which immediately present the hardships of a singular life in the way that the Book of Ruth does in the Bible. In a handful of verses and by the end of the short first chapter, loss and despair and self-pity and uncertainty about the future are all laid out in head-shaking detail regarding Naomi's nearly unimaginably painful years in Moab. She was so hurt that when she returned to her homeland of Bethlehem, "empty" as she described it, she insisted that she be called a name meaning "bitter" and "afflicted."

In similar fashion, these relatively few pages of the testimony of Susie Gladney-Lee are instantly captivating and demand your empathy, imagination, and curiosity. But so too will you be led to join Susie in celebration regarding what she appropriately describes as her God-given triumph over tragedy. There is pain and healing in the truth that you will find in this book.

While Susie doesn't talk much, she is talking more now than she ever has. She often comes off as uncomfortable in a crowd. It's almost as if she doesn't want to be seen or, perhaps more likely, it is because she has too often been seen in a dehumanizing way by sick individuals whose conduct was criminal in some instances and uncaring in others. Yes, she's talking more now. Her voice is becoming exponentially stronger each day. So too is her resolve to understand for herself, and make clear to others, that she has been victimized but must refuse to be a victim. She no longer believes, like she once did, that she "was just born to endure pain and die."

Author Sandra Marinella wrote, "In facing our shattered life stories, we must reach deep inside our pain-for it is here that we can break our silence and find our new voice."

In this day when literacy has dramatically improved, Susie states, without further explanation, that she cannot read nor write. But that has not stopped her. She gave this testimony to a friend and asked her to make it available to the rest of us. Her story is impactful as you will soon find. Her spirit as an overcomer is evident in every paragraph.

Susie tells us that she repeatedly saw a vision of a tangled ball of yarn. In these pages, she pulls on the string for us and communicates God's love and a plan of peace and purpose for our lives just as clearly as does the writer of the Book of Ruth. That story, like Susie's, ends with the image of Naomi surrounded by new life and friends who declared that God was a "restorer" of her life.

Celebrated author and civil rights activist, Maya Angelou,

whose early life story has similarities to Susie's, famously declared that she reached a point when she knew why the caged bird sings. Angelou is not the only one who learned the secret of such birds under those circumstances. Susie Gladney-Lee knows the secret too.

While it has been a long time coming, there is much greater attention to imposing legal consequences upon perpetrators of violence against women. Shocking stories of brutality, sexual assault and death fill the pages of newspapers and shatter lives. It takes courage for those who are being and have been victimized to fight back in various ways, including exposing those who have hurt them. Telling their stories is often a first step to reclaiming what the abusers thought they had taken.

Susie is one such courageous person. Her candid detailing of the trauma inflicted on her as a child, throughout her marriage, and well into her adulthood will, sadly, be familiar to some who read her story. For those who see themselves and a bit of their own lives in this story, take the steps now to preserve your life. Report the abuse. Find safe refuge for you and your children. Seek criminal prosecution for stalking, harassment and assault.

As Susie's long-time pastor and a friend, I am in awe of her growing confidence in her "somebodyness." She is a faithful Christian and a daily inspiration to all of us. She gives God the glory for the things He has done.

Finally, as you read these vignettes about her life, there will be times that you will be forced to read about an episode one more time just to confirm that you read what you thought you read. On other occasions your mouth will fly open. And, for some of the text, you will shut your eyes tightly and leave them closed as you first try to image the situation and then desperately hope that you can get the images out of your head. But if all that you get out of this book are what Susie recounts about the mistreatment and heartache and disappointment, then you will have missed the ultimate point. You should also see that weeping may endure for a night, but joy comes in the morning.

Author Susie Gladney-Lee, we see you. Thank you for trusting us by being transparent and for trusting yourself enough to summon your voice. We hear you too.

Reverend Orlando R. Richmond, Sr.
Northside Christian Church
West Point, Mississippi
July 3, 2024

1

A BALL OF YARN

As I sit here in this moment, my mind goes back to when I was a little girl and my mom would do my hair. She would put all those little plaits on my head, and they'd be sticking up everywhere. She made sure we went to church, even if she didn't go. We would have to walk to church, but we didn't care. I loved to hear singing. Even now, I still love to hear that old time gospel singing, it always takes me back to the days of my youth. My youth wasn't all that perfect, but now as I reflect back, even then God had a purpose for me. I never would have thought that God would use my life for His purpose, but here I am. I am still here and God is using all of my pain for purpose, all of my test for testimonies, turned all of my worries into worship and my depression to expression. I finally have the chance to express myself.

No I can't read or write, but I still have a voice. I have never really talked much because it seems I was always silenced. All of my heartaches, pains, trials and tribulations were muted. I was just existing. How I felt, never mattered to anyone, but little did I know, it mattered to God! I mattered to God! When I felt like I was just born to endure pain and die, God had another plan for me. People had counted me out, but God had counted me in. Who would have ever thought that I would have the courage to tell my story. We all have a story to tell if people would take the time and listen. My Pastor told me when I first joined their church, that I had a story to tell. He was absolutely right. I had so many things bottled up inside of me until I felt like it was choking me out. My life was just full of twists and turns, tangled up in a ball. I didn't know how to unravel it right then, but as time went on the Lord began to show me, He would do it strand by strand.

I'm reminded of Mama Etta Tucker, rest her sweet soul, she always looked out for me. I remember the day that I told her that I wanted to work in the church. I told her that I kept seeing this white robe just hanging over the water, and then I would see Jesus's face. His hair was brown and his arms were stretched wide. I felt chills all over my body. I didn't know what it meant, but Mama Etta told me that my calling was to be an Usher.

Mama Etta got me on the Usher's Ministry. I ushered for about nine years. I felt so good about what I was doing. I remember the first time I wore my blue uniform, I never wanted to take it off. It felt so good to serve others. Walking up and down those aisles attending to God's people. I was doing something worthwhile, something that made me proud of myself.

Later I joined another church, and ooooh what a change that took place in my life! The **Word** was like eating something brand new that I had never tasted before. As the Pastor was breaking the bread of life, I ate with understanding. I had never heard the word being broken down like this before. It felt so good, reminds me of the scripture, O Taste and See that the Lord is good. This Pastor, Rev. Orlando Richmond, broke the word down so that even babies could understand. Other churches I had gone to had great service, great speakers, but when I heard this Pastor, this man of God, it opened my understanding. This is where I belonged. My friend and I joined the Usher's Ministry.

I was an usher here for about ten years and then my legs begin to bother me and I couldn't stand as long. It really bothered me that I couldn't do my usher duties, because this ministry was so dear to me. I had been asking God what did He want me to do since I could no longer usher.

Then the Lord kept showing me visions of a ball of yarn. Every morning I shared it with my friend, and the more I talked about it, the more my understanding began to open up. My friend begin to encourage me to share my vision of the strands of yarn with the world.

Each strand of yarn represented different strands in my life. BUT JESUS is my Lifeline. Whatever I needed or need,

A TANGLED BALL OF YARN

He has never let me down. As He kept showing me the ball of yarn, I began to see my life and experiences in every strand. My family, my health, my relationships, my past hurts and pains and my connection to Him were all wrapped up like a ball of yarn. I began to realize that HE WAS THE LIFELINE in the midst of all the yarn, no matter how they were tangled or crossed up....HE IS THE ONLY ONE THAT CAN STRAIGHTEN IT OUT.

2

SACRIFICES

In order to sacrifice, there has to be love. There is no love without sacrifice.

As we rode on the van heading to the clubhouse, I began to laugh. I remembered the time when one of my daughters, my niece and I were out exercising. We took a walk, just laughing and talking. And then all of a sudden, out of nowhere, a mad dog came running fast, and barking loud and vicious! Looord, there was no where to go! And if it was a place to go, I couldn't get there fast enough because I couldn't run! My daughter was yelling,

"Come on Momma" and she was running for her life, as well as my niece she was on the run too.

"Susie! Susie! Come on!" They were running and looking back at me. But there was no run in me. I told them, "Ruuuuun! Run on! He can eat me!" I didn't even try. I was going to let the dog eat me so that they could get away. I told them, "Yall run on cause I ain't running!"

But then, I tried to run just a little bit. They ran on and got the truck and pulled up. I was dragging at this point. The dog had looked at me, and turned and went the other way. All that for nothing!

Now when I think about this incident, I laugh and think about how fun and exciting it was at the time, even though it was terrifying. I was willing to sacrifice my own life for my family. God did it best when He sent His only begotten Son Jesus to die for us. God did it because He loves us.

When I was thirteen, I had to make a sacrifice and only the Lord knows it hurt me so bad when I had to give my own child up. My mom kept telling me that I was too young and that I didn't know what to do with a baby. Talking about a deep hurt, this took my breath away.

At this age, my ball of yarn had already started to ball up, this was just another hurtful thing that had happened in my life. I couldn't explain to anyone how I felt because it didn't matter to anyone. They just kept saying I was too young to take care of a baby.

The pain felt like someone ripping my skin from my body, but what could I do? I was only a child that had to live under someone else's rules. Even though they felt like they were doing the right thing for me, and my baby, it didn't stop the pain in my heart. It didn't stop my heart from bleeding pain. Because that's all I felt. I couldn't figure out at my age why I had to face so much hurt and I wasn't even an adult yet.

My mom was so mad about the pregnancy, she kept asking,

"Whose baby is this? Who did this to you?"

I couldn't say a word because I already knew she was about to whip me good either way, so I just kept quiet. I just took it for me and my child's father. We didn't even know what we were doing. Because of other things that had already happened to me when I was younger, I had mastered keeping quiet, it kept other people out of trouble, but it kept me full of pain, fear and even rage.

What a world of pain I was born into, and in my mind, I wondered if this pain would ever go away. If I had known that things were only going to get worse from here, I don't know if I could have kept breathing.

The hurt and love of family can run so deep. And sometimes you don't have the liberty to speak on it. It just balls up into the ball of yarn, and my little hands couldn't unravel it.

3

TEARS

God was showing me this ball of yarn, the ball is tangled, just like life is. No matter how I tried to unravel it, I messed it up even more. Each string represents something pertaining to my life. I guess that's why I keep saying that God is the Lifeline, JESUS is my Lifeline.

I can't untangle it, my family and friends can't untangle it, but in God's Hands, He is slowly untangling things in His own time. I was trying, but I don't have the same patience as God, I began to get frustrated. I was only making things bigger than they were....But God has a slow merciful hand.

Even now as an adult, I still shed tears, like just today, I couldn't grasp in my mind, how a grown man could take advantage of a four year old baby.

I was four years old when my parents moved out of state to live with one of my family members. Boy did my parents love him. My dad went to work in a wine vineyard everyday and my mom did other odds and end jobs, and I had no one to play with. I was the only child at that time. But my cousin would take it upon himself to relieve my mother. He would tell her he was taking me to the store to get ice cream, but little to my surprise, this was not the treat I was looking for.

My cousin was a perverted man. He would take me in the store, buy me ice cream, and then take me to an alley to eat it and then he would do horrible things to me. I would cry so loud! There was no one to save me from my nice cousin. He would tell me to be quiet, be a big girl and not tell my parents because they would be mad at me. After he was done with me, he would clean me up and take me back to his house, where my parent's lived with him. I would cry when my daddy went to work. I would beg my daddy to let me go and help him, but he always said I was too little to stay home with my mom and cousin. No one knew what I was dealing with.

Things changed, my cousin took me to the store one day, and told me to get all the candy I wanted. I already knew what he was going to do to me. I got the candy and when we left the store and went to the alley, there was a man standing there smiling at us. He was waiting for me. He took my hand and my cousin followed behind us smiling. We went into an apartment not far from that alley and this man that I didn't know, did all types of sexual things to me as if I were an adult. When he was done, this stranger gave me a bath and led me back to my cousin. My cousin stopped, got me ice cream, and then back to his home, where we lived with him. I could not believe this, who would listen to me? My cousin said they would be mad at me. I cried every time they allowed me to leave with him, but he would pick me up and say,

"Let's get you some chips and ice cream, you love that!"

Who would save me? When will help come? My cousin and this man had taken my life and no one knows it but me. My tears now flow on the inside as well as on the outside. No one knows what I am feeling and I can't tell them. I just want this to stop, but who can stop it? All I have are my tears and no one sees them. I still shed tears about this but God wipes them.

I should not have been treated this way as a baby. But now I realize that if my parents had known they would have saved me. I was just too afraid to speak up because my cousin said they would be mad at me. I had learned to be quiet, and just take the pain, in silence. A loud silence.

God has seen my tears and heard me cry, I don't know a proper prayer but I know God understands what I am saying. God will heal me and restore me in His own time. I have never shared this with anyone but my friend that's been encouraging me to speak about this yarn and it does feel better to get it out finally. The more I talk about this, it seems like my load is shedding. I'm slowly getting rid of this heavy load. Thank You Lord!

Sometimes you have to use your voice to set your mind free. Whom the Son sets free, is free indeed. Glory to God, I am free, indeed!

4

FAMILY STRINGS PULL HARD

Family strings are the most delicate, but they pull harder than any other string because they are pulling straight from the heart.

The good Lord bless me with two beautiful daughters and often times they are the reason I cry the most. My family isn't the way I want it to be and there are so many things that happened to destroy me that it leaked into my family, because they are just an extension of me, they are ME. I've been trying so long to unravel the twisted and tangled up strings from around my family, the harder I try, the more resistant things get. It seems like even though I am trying to make it work, I am only making it worse.

It's so hard to walk away from family and let the Lord have it. I cry tears of sorrow, thinking about the way it should be, and to see that it is so far from that, all because of the division that took place when I was thirteen. I had no control over my mother's decision. But that decision has felt like a curse! It has been like a driving force to keep my family divided. I have no more apologies. I have apologized all that I could. I have tried to explain my side the best that I possibly can, I have extended my love as far as it could possibly go. I have done all that I have had power to do but it wasn't enough to unravel what had started when I was a little girl.

My mind goes back to the question, will this pain ever go away? I became tired and I felt defeated when it came to trying to bind my family together. I decided to let go because I was too weak to continue. My heart kept taking blow after blow. The enemy, that old Satan is having a field day with my life, with my family. But God begin to move....the very wad of yarn that is out of control to me, He grabbed one string and begin to straighten it out in HIS own time. I can slowly see a light that I didn't see before. I am cautious, I don't want to mess it up. I just want God to get the glory. I can see His hands pulling that knot out of the ball for me. The very one I've been pulling on for years, in just a matter of months, He is doing it.

I love both my daughters so much. I love them equally and in their own way. Circumstances pulled us apart but it's my FAITH in God that is helping us find our way back together. What the enemy meant to destroy me, being quiet and always taking the fall for people, this time, I'm using my voice! I am standing up for myself first of all, and then I stand up for my own two daughters.

I didn't get to raise you two together the way I wanted to but only God knows why He allows, what He allows and I trust Him. Even though I don't understand the process, I still trust God, and give God the Glory in this. I have confidence that it will work out the way God has planned it.

5

LIVING WITH TWO MEN

I think back when I met this man loving, sweet, gentle, a provider, he was all of that to me. He could really cook. He was a chef, my chef. He could do anything as far I could see. His family loved him, his daughter adored him and me, well I allowed him to be my whole world.

I felt like he loved me so much, until he just wanted me all to himself. Every woman wants security. But sometimes security for us is a life sentence. I had given all of me because Lord knows, I wanted to be loved back. My husband, when he was man number one, he was the best thing alive. But when he was man number two, he was the most meanest thing alive.

I lived in the same neighborhood as my parents and couldn't see them. My husband was so jealous. I could only be in the presence of his parents and family. I became like a daughter to his mom and dad, having to forsake my own family, just to keep the peace. I cried many nights, being so close to my own mom and dad and could not see them, but yet I waited on his parents everyday hand and foot.

I loved his mom, everywhere she went, I had to go not because she wanted me to, but because her son would have a heart attack if for a moment he thought I was alone. This obsession of his was breathtaking, literally, I felt like I couldn't breathe any more. I no longer had a life of my own.

Childhood to adulthood had become a waste for me. If it wasn't for being cursed out, being punched and pushed around, being shot at, I wasn't living. What was my life? I lived with my stomach in knots. Everyday I anticipated which man was coming to the house. Would it be man number one, that would kill a squirrel, rabbit, deer or coon and come in clean it, and cook it and make me feel good to be around him? Or would it be man number 2, that would stagger in and hit me with his empty bottle and yell at me to do this or to do that?

One night everyone was running and I didn't know what was going on, My daddy-in-law yelled my name,

"Susie you better run, he finna shoot you!"

I panicked, I froze! I heard the gunshot, it went passed my head. I made up in my mind. I gotta get out of this. I got me a ticket. I was getting out of town. I couldn't do it anymore. I was full. I had taken all that I could. Even though his family loved me, they were loyal to him. They told him. And he came and got me and my baby from the train station, and told me that I wasn't taking his baby anywhere. Like a sheep before the slaughter. I was in bondage again.

A TANGLED BALL OF YARN

Years were moving and I was still in the same place, gasping for air. This made me think about the fish that his mom would catch on the pool bank. They would lay there fighting for their life at first, flapping and jumping trying to get back in the water, and then they would just give up and GASP for air. I had accepted that it wasn't going to change for me or get any better for me or my daughter. I finally gave up and stop fighting, stop trying to leave and just gave in to prayer. It didn't get any better, it was the same. One thing I knew was that my husband whichever man he was, loved me. He was so afraid I would leave him, until he threatened me not to leave him-even though I had never mentioned it. We had some good times that didn't outnumber the bad.

My husband began telling people that he was going to die when he turned 47. I begged him to stop saying that. My marriage wasn't perfect, but I didn't want to be a widow either. Time continued to move on without me, I was still in the same place.

One morning, with my husband's arms wrapped around me, my youngest daughter came into the room, it was time to get her ready for school. I wasn't able to wake my husband or to pry his arms from around me. We called his name and continued to try to pry him off only to find out, that even in death, he wouldn't let me go.

He left me. I'm not sure what time he left, but instead of me finding a way to leave him, he left me first. I still wonder about that to this day, how when we let go, God moves.

I was married to one husband but he was two different

men. I am not trying to act like he was a bad man or anything, but some of the things I had to endure were not great. Even though he loved me, sometimes I had to wonder did I love myself.

I stood by him through sickness, drunkenness, soberness, wellness. I endured many things to be by his side. When he was in the hospital, I was there every waking moment. I remember one of his brothers trying to persuade him to let him stay, so that I could go home and see about our daughter. I needed to get a good bath and change of clothes but he wasn't having it. He was so afraid I was going to leave him. But when it was all said and done, he was the one that left me behind. My husband left me.

I loved that man. Even in the bad, he was still good to me, that was just the way that he loved me.

6

A VISIT FROM HELL

My life changed so fast. I went from being a wife to a widow. I was so used to being controlled until I felt like a bird that had been caged for so long, that I wasn't sure how to fly away when it was time to. When my husband passed on, I lived with other family members until I was able to move on my own.

I had finally moved into my own place, I didn't really call it home because it was an apartment that I knew would never be mine. I was asking God for a home. I wanted a brick home and that was my constant prayer.

Even though, I wasn't where I wanted to be yet, I was still on a high about being an usher. I was proud to wear that usher's uniform. I was dropped off in front of the apartments where I lived after a revival service. My head was held high, because I had my uniform on. I walked proud. I was a servant and I loved every minute of it. Sometimes I didn't want to take that uniform off, it made me feel like somebody special.

People even looked at me different all because I was a door keeper in the house of the Lord.

That night while walking to my apartment, I passed another lady's apartment as well and there sat two men drinking. They spoke to me before I got to them and I spoke back. One of the men went on and on about how nice I looked in my usher uniform. He got up and said that he needed to walk me to my apartment so that nothing would happen to me. I told him I was fine, I didn't need an escort, but he continued to follow me. And he kept saying things that he shouldn't have been saying. While unlocking my door, I asked him to leave, but he would not. When I had unlocked my door he pushed his way in. And pulled me in as well.

I kept asking him to please leave but he wouldn't. I knew this was not going to be a good ending, so I started begging him to leave my apartment.

He grabbed me and pulled my skirt off. I cried, trying to hold on to his hands but he was so drunk and so strong. He continued pulling off my uniform skirt. I knew this was the devil, just evil. He didn't stop until he had pushed me down and got on top of me. I could smell the alcohol, his sweat and most of all the pain that he was thrusting on me. I thought I was going to die. This demon had pulled off my uniform, and now it felt like he was ripping my insides. I was so scared. When he was done, he just laughed at me, fixed his clothes and left me lying there in fear and pain. I couldn't move. I couldn't believe this had happened to me, I was in my uniform, that was now defiled and wrinkled. My life was ripped, wrinkled and just worn down. I finally got up and locked my door. I was so scared. My body was wreaking with pain. Who could I tell? Nobody. I made up my mind to just keep silent.

Different circumstances took place and my Karate Instructor saw a drastic change in me, I couldn't stop crying. He continued trying to figure out what had took place. He got one of my cousins that was also in the class with me and they wouldn't stop until I finally broke.

They rushed me to the Emergency Room to be checked, the police was called. But because I had taken a bath, they said there was no evidence. Even with giving them the name and where he lived, there was no evidence. Again....silence.

I was living in fear. He lived in walking distance from my apartment. I was too afraid to leave home, and too afraid to come back home after I had left. My life was caged up again, bondage. I was living peeping through blinds and peeping out of doors before I left home. I would never walk on the front of my apartment again. I always left and came in through the back, I was afraid he would see me. I could hear his voice sitting in front of his mom's house. Hearing his laughter and loud voice, gave me chills and made my heart race. I was moving fast not to be seen by him.

Time went on and a few people found out what had happened to me, and they were upset that nothing was done. He finally moved to live with his girlfriend, which gave me a little peace. People were telling me his every move. They knew I was living in fear. Until one day someone stopped by to tell me that his girlfriend had killed him.

Honestly, it was at that moment, that I took a deep breath and cried. My stomach was relieved. My mind had been relieved. No one knew what type of hell this man had put me in. That revival night visit from hell had changed my life. I had lived in fear all my life, people were just taking, taking, taking and taking from me. No one was giving, giving, giving. But when I heard those words, he was dead, the breath came back into my body. My heart went out to his mother. She had no idea what her son had done to me, or how he had put my whole life in a cage. I felt sorry for her. But I was so relieved that he couldn't hurt me again.

7

THE LORD IS MY SHEPHERD

I didn't get an education. I didn't get a perfect life. But I will admit, I've got the perfect God. Out of all the things I went through, God never left me. I could have easily given up and in some situations I did give up, because I was tired. But God kept me!

One morning I was sitting waiting on my ride and I could see a pretty green pasture and there was nothing on it, just beautiful green grass like carpet. And I thought about the 23 Psalm, the Lord is my Shepherd. He has always led me, even when I didn't know it.

I didn't want to live in those apartments and after the visit from hell, I certainly didn't want to live there any more. But the Lord answered my prayer. My daughter saw the brick house and made some calls, got everything set up for me and I was able to move into my brick home. Even while living here in the home that I prayed for, I have still dealt with issues but God.

I thought about the day my air went out and it was over the holidays, I couldn't get anyone to come and fix my air, it was so hot in the house, that my son-in-law came and got me to get me out of the heat. When I came back home the next day, someone came and fixed my air. I asked did my daughter send him and he told me, no. I asked did the place I pay mortgage to send him, he said no. He just got orders to come here and repair the air. My daughter knew nothing of it, and my mortgage place was still closed for the holidays. I asked what did I owe, and he said it was already covered. The Lord is my Shepherd!

I remember telling my friend that encouraged me to write the book that my yard needed to be cut really bad but I didn't have the money. She is a witness that I came home from the program and a guy that I didn't know was cutting my grass. I stopped him and asked him who sent him because I didn't have any money. He asked me was I Mrs. Dale? I said no sir baby, "I am Susie Lee" I said the Dales live across the street. He said, "Well I'm cutting the wrong yard." He said, "Well this is on me, and since I've cut this side I might as well finish now. The Lord is my Shepherd.

He didn't bring me this far to leave me now. I give God all the Glory for raising me back up out of a sea of hurt, depression, oppression, pain, heartache, fear, molestation, rape and silence. I could have lost my mind but the Lord is my Shepherd.

8

TRIUMPH OVER TRAGEDY

As I take time and reflect back on my trials, tribulations, heartaches, pains, and misunderstandings, I realize that I didn't make it on my own. I'm a witness that God gave me Triumph Over Tragedy.

What came to take me out, had no power over me...I prevailed, all because of God. Before someone leaves my story feeling sad, mad, or sorry for me, before you leave this book feeling like maybe I shouldn't have told this or that, this is my voice that has never been heard.

I lived every bit of what you've read and more. You read my story but you still can't feel the pain that I felt and some of the pain that I still feel. I still shed tears, I still see my experiences from time to time. But praise the Lord with me that He brought me out, so that you will know that whatever you are facing, GOD IS ABLE to bring you out!

As a baby, so many babies get abused and die from it, but God kept me. And God is still keeping me right now. I've had many ups and downs, feels like more downs than ups, but the upside is GOD is with me. I've been mistreated, but I can tell you that, you will be OK. I've been criticized and talked about, dogged out, labeled but all of that just to tell someone else that you will survive it!

My story is not a glorious one but God gets the GLORY!

Every obstacle in my path, the Lord always caused me to triumph over it. Yes Jesus loves me. He showed me when He gave His very life for me. As I became a born again believer, He has never left my side. At this age, I've never seen the righteous forsaken nor His seed begging for bread, I know what David means now.

The marriage was rough at times but I made it. I lost my husband, it hurt so bad, still hurts but I'm still here. I survived that!

The rape hurt me mentally, physically, emotionally and socially, but I'm still here. I think about it, but it no longer has power over me.

When I was a little girl being taken advantage of and nobody knew it but me and God. He still kept me intact. He could have let me been taken out in that alley, killed, missing and never returned to my parents, but GOD.

My daughter being taken away from me at the age of thirteen, what an indescribable pain, but we are both still here. Only God knows why He allows what He allows. We shouldn't even question God, just thank Him that He saw something in us that He was able to use for His glory, to demonstrate His redeeming power.

There is nobody like God!

AFTERWORD

I met Susie in November of 2017. It was during the first few months on my job. She approached me at a Thanksgiving gathering and inquired about attending the elderly program where I was the program manager. I immediately said yes because I was recruiting new clients at the time. Months went by and she noticed me again at a Shell gas station and asked again. I then went to work and got her approved to attend my program. Over the years, through building a rapport with her we have gained each other's trust. After reading her story, I am in awe of her perseverance and determination to not allow what she has gone through break her. I hope her story gives someone who may be faced with the same situations she did the courage to speak up and tell someone. I hope it also helps them to heal and grow into the person they desire to be. Susie is not what she's gone through but more of what she's overcome. She is nurturing and passionate about those that she loves. This book depicts how despite what she endured her thoughts were always about mothering her kids and helping others.

I'm happy our paths crossed years ago, because I've gotten to witness the layers pulled back and see her and the voice she's always been searching for.

-Christon Robinson

Author Susie Gladney-Lee

Susie born and raised in rural Clay County, MS. She is the mother of two beautiful daughters and has beautiful grands and a great grand. Family is dear to Susie. Susie is a member of the North Side Christian Church where she attends faithfully. Susie has a fondness for creating things. She is a hands on person.

She loves the Lord and gives Him all the glory for every situation in her life.